# WARM-BLOODED ANIMALS

# Curriculum Consultants

Dr. Arnold L. Willems
Associate Professor of Curriculum and Instruction
The University of Wyoming

Dr. Gerald W. Thompson
Associate Professor
Social Studies Education
Old Dominion University

Dr. Dale Rice
Associate Professor
Department of Elementary and Early Childhood Education
University of South Alabama

Dr. Fred Finley
Assistant Professor of Science Education
University of Wisconsin

# Subject Area Consultants

**Astronomy**
Robert Burnham
Associate Editor
*Astronomy* Magazine and *Odyssey* Magazine

**Geology**
Dr. Norman P. Lasca
Professor of Geology
University of Wisconsin — Milwaukee

**Oceanography**
William MacLeish
Editor
*Oceanus* Magazine

**Paleontology**
Linda West
Dinosaur National Monument
Jensen, Utah

**Physiology**
Kirk Hogan, M.D.
Madison, Wisconsin

**Sociology/Anthropology**
Dr. Arnold Willems
Associate Professor of Curriculum and Instruction
College of Education
University of Wyoming

**Technology**
Dr. Robert T. Balmer
Professor of Mechanical Engineering
University of Wisconsin — Milwaukee

**Transportation**
James A. Knowles
Division of Transportation
Smithsonian Institution

Irving Birnbaum
Air and Space Museum
Smithsonian Institution

Donald Berkebile
Division of Transportation
Smithsonian Institution

**Zoology**
Dr. Carroll R. Norden
Professor of Zoology
University of Wisconsin —
  Milwaukee

First published in Great Britain by Macmillan Children's
  Books, a division of Macmillan Publishers Ltd, under the
  title *Look It Up*.
First edition copyright © 1979, 1981 Macmillan Publishers Ltd
  (for volumes 1-10)
First edition copyright © 1980, 1981 Macmillan Publishers Ltd
  (for volumes 11-16)
Second edition copyright © 1985, 1986 Macmillan Publishers Ltd

Published in the United States of America

Text this edition copyright © 1986 Raintree Publishers Inc.

Library of Congress Number: 86-649

2 3 4 5 6 7 8 9 0    90 89 88

Printed and bound in the United States of America.

**Library of Congress Cataloging-in-Publication Data**

Let's discover warm-blooded animals.

  (Let's discover; 1)
  Bibliography: p. 70
  Includes index.
  Summary: A reference book dealing with birds and specific
mammal groups such as rodents, carnivores, and ungulates.
  1. Mammals—Juvenile literature. 2. Birds—Juvenile
literature. [1. Mammals. 2. Birds] I. Title: Warm-blooded
animals. II. Series.
AG6.L43   1986 vol. 1   [QL706.2]   031s   [599]   86-649
ISBN 0-8172-2600-1 (lib. bdg.)
ISBN 0-8172-2581-1 (softcover)

# LET'S DISCOVER
# WARM-BLOODED ANIMALS

## RAINTREE PUBLISHERS
Milwaukee

# Contents

# WARM-BLOODED ANIMALS

Mammals and birds are warm-blooded animals. Their bodies stay at about the same temperature all the time. Mammals have fur or hair and birds have feathers to help keep them warm. People wear heavy clothes in winter to keep warm.

shrew

hedgehog

mole

dormouse

squirrels

bats

squirrel

wood mouse

rabbit

rabbit

rabbits

badgers

# BIRDS

Birds are the only animals that have feathers. Their feathers keep them warm and dry. They also help them to fly. Birds fly by moving their wings up and down. Their tails help them turn in the air. Their bodies are very light.

The European robin has a pointed beak that can pick up insects.

All birds lay eggs. The eggs must be kept warm by the parent birds. A baby bird will grow inside each egg. After the chicks break out of the eggshells, the parents care for them until they can fly.

Hawks have a hooked beak that can tear meat apart.

Birds use their beaks to hold things, to build nests, and for eating. They do not have teeth.

The hawfinch has a very strong beak for splitting seeds.

Birds live in nests. The nest keeps the eggs and baby birds safe. Birds make nests in different ways. Some make round nests on the twigs of a tree or bush.

Woodpeckers make holes in tree trunks. Other birds dig holes in the ground. Many birds make nests of grass on top of the ground.

blackbird

weaver bird

woodpecker

teal

hummingbird

# Tree birds

Many birds live in trees. Some live in nests on the branches. Others live in holes in the tree trunk. Birds find food in trees. They eat the fruit, flowers, and leaves. They also catch insects that live on leaves.

This spotted woodpecker lives in a hole in a tree trunk. It holds on to the bark with its claws.

Brightly colored parrots live in warm, wet forests. Their favorite foods are nuts, fruit and seeds.

Birds of paradise live in the hot forests of Australia and New Guinea. The males have beautiful feathers.

This crested pigeon is guarding its chicks. These baby birds will stay in the nest until they can fly. The parents take turns to bring them food.

ostrich

# Ground birds

Some birds stay mostly on the ground. That is where they find their food. The turkey eats insects and berries on the ground. It sleeps in a tree at night. But it cannot fly far. The ostrich cannot fly at all. It has very small wings. Ostriches can run very fast.

turkey

These birds lived long ago. None of them can be found now. They were large and could not fly.

dodo        moa        diatryma

The male peacock opens his fan
of beautiful feathers to attract a
female. She is called a peahen.
Peahens do not have those
brightly colored feathers.

This kiwi lives in New Zealand.
It has tiny wings that are hidden
under its feathers. Kiwis come
out at night to look for worms.

# Birds of prey

Birds that hunt and eat other animals are called birds of prey. Their sharp claws catch their prey. Their hooked beaks tear the prey apart. Mostly they catch living animals. But vultures eat dead animals.

The osprey eats only fish. When it sees a fish, it dives feet-first into the water. It catches the fish with its long claws.

The goshawk lives in forests. It hunts birds. It can move quickly through the trees. This helps it to catch its prey.

snowy owl

lemming

The snowy owl lives in the Arctic. Its feathers help it to hide in the ice and snow. Most owls hunt at night. But the snowy owl hunts lemmings, its prey, in the daytime.

The barn owl usually hunts at night. But if its family needs extra food, it will also hunt in the daytime.

## Seabirds

Some seabirds dive from high places to catch fish. The gannet is such a bird. Others dive from the surface of the water. Gulls, terns, and fulmars stay near land. The albatross hunts far from land.

puffin

Puffins live in holes in cliffs. They swim underwater to catch fish. They carry fish in their large beaks.

fulmar

common gull

kittiwakes

wandering albatross

shags

herring gull

Seabirds make their nests on cliffs and beaches. Kittiwakes make nests of seaweed high on the cliffs.

roseate tern

Arctic tern

gannet

17

# Swans, ducks, and geese

Ducks, geese, and swans are called waterfowl. Their webbed feet help them to swim. Oil on their feathers keeps them dry in the water. Swans are the largest waterfowl. Ducks are the smallest. Swans and ducks find their food underwater. Geese feed on land.

The shoveler uses its broad beak to get food from mud.

Many geese make their nests in the far north. Then they fly south to live where it is warm in winter. Flocks of geese often form a V shape in the air. A flock of geese on the ground is called a gaggle.

The merganser's beak has tiny hooks for holding fish.

The mallard eats small insects and plants.

Swans always land on water. They push out their feet to help them slow down on the water.

Ducks often flock together in winter. In the picture you can see mallards and pintails.

# Long-legged birds

Some water birds do not swim very often. Instead, they use their long legs to wade in the water. Their long necks and beaks help them to find food in the water. They like to eat plants that grow in lakes and swamps. The water there is still and the food easy to see.

Storks are long-legged. They build their nests on chimney tops. Some people think it is lucky to have a stork's nest on the house.

gray heron

The flamingo is a long-legged bird that lives in large groups in warm places. These birds have longer necks than any other bird. They hold their beaks upside down in the water to feed on tiny plants and animals.

Cranes are the largest long-legged birds. Some cranes fly to warm places in winter. Herons also do this. All the birds in this picture feed on fish and other water animals.

crane

stork

# MAMMALS

There are 5,000 kinds of mammals. The mammals in this picture live in forests in South America. Some of them spend their time in the trees. Other mammals, such as the agouti, live in holes under the ground. Giant otters swim in the rivers and eat fish. Bats fly through the air. Jaguars hunt tapirs and other animals.

bat

sloth

titi monkeys

spider monkey

tapir

jaguar

agouti

giant otter

Baby mammals feed on milk from their mother's body. No other animals feed their babies this way. Some baby mammals are helpless when they are born. Their mothers must keep them warm. Other baby mammals, such as piglets, are not so helpless.

duck-billed platypus

Two kinds of mammals lay eggs. All other mammals have baby mammals. The duck-billed platypus and the echidna lay eggs. They both live in Australia and New Guinea.

koalas

Some mammals keep their babies in a kind of pocket, called a pouch. The koala is such a mammal. A baby koala is less than an inch long at birth.

# Pouched mammals

Pouched mammals carry their babies in a large pocket called a pouch. Such mammals live mostly in Australia. Kangaroos, wallabies, and koalas are pouched mammals. They are related to the opossums of America. Many pouched mammals look like other mammals.

When a baby kangaroo is born, it is very tiny. It crawls through its mother's fur and into her pouch. It stays there until it is bigger.

Bilbys live in holes in the ground. They come out at night to eat insects. They are also called bandicoots.

Kangaroos hop with both legs together. They leap as far and as high as athletes.

The scrub wallaby is a small kangaroo that can hop very fast.

# Monkeys and apes

Monkeys and apes nearly all live in forests. They climb trees, using their hands and feet to hold on to branches. Some monkeys can hang by their tails. Baboons live on the ground. But they will climb trees when they are afraid. Monkeys eat mainly fruit and leaves.

mandrill

olive baboon

howler monkey

bonnet monkey

marmoset

There are four kinds of apes. They are the gorilla, the chimpanzee, the gibbon, and the orangutan.

Apes do not have tails. They are very intelligent. Gibbons and orangutans use their long arms to swing through the trees.

gorilla

chimpanzee

gibbon

orangutan

# GNAWING MAMMALS

Many mammals gnaw their food. Some of these mammals are called rodents. The best known rodents are rats and mice.

Rodents have long, sharp front teeth. When they gnaw food like nuts and roots, they wear down their teeth. But a rodent's teeth grow as fast as they wear down.

Rabbits and hares are gnawing animals. But they are not rodents. They have an extra pair of front teeth that rodents do not have.

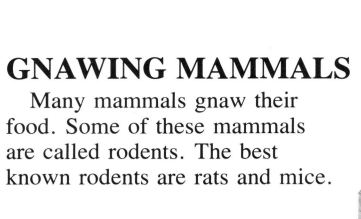

hamster

jerboa

gerbil

Hamsters, gerbils, and jerboas are all rodents. Hamsters and gerbils are kept as pets. Wild gerbils and jerboas live in deserts. They drink little water.

beaver

A beaver can cut down trees with its teeth. It eats the bark of the trees. It uses the trunk and branches to build a dam in a river. When a pond forms behind the dam, the beaver builds its home with twigs and branches in the pond.

Squirrels are rodents. They eat nuts and berries. They build nests in high trees. They are good climbers and can jump from branch to branch. Their bushy tails help them do this.

# Rats and mice

There are many different kinds of rats and mice. Most of them are harmless. A few kinds are pests. Animals become pests when they live in large numbers and cause damage. Rats and mice eat our crops and spread diseases. They live in nests under the ground. They are very shy so we hardly ever see them.

The harvest mouse is different. It builds its nest above ground. It fastens the nest to plant stems. It likes to live in wheat fields.

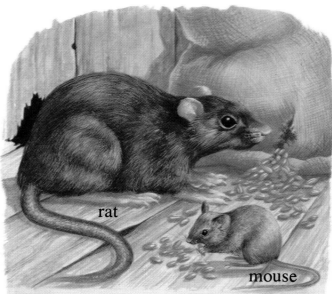

rat

mouse

The black rat and house mouse are pests. They live in houses and barns. They eat grain and other foods.

# Rabbits and hares

Rabbits and hares are different from rodents. Rabbits and hares have long ears, long legs, and short tails. Baby rabbits are born blind. But baby hares are born with their eyes open.

jack rabbit

Arctic hare

Rabbits and hares lose body heat through their ears. The jack rabbit lives in the desert. Its extra long ears help it to keep cool. The Arctic hare has small ears. It does not lose much heat in the cold air.

rabbits

# SEA MAMMALS

Seals, sea lions, and walruses are mammals that live in the sea. They come to shore to have their babies and to rest. They swim well but are clumsy on land. Sea lions and walruses can move on land quite fast by holding up their back flippers.

The walruses shown here use their tusks to dig for food.

The picture below shows a baby gray seal with its mother. The baby is called a pup. It can swim when it is three weeks old.

This diver is wearing flippers. They help him to swim like the sea lion. The diver gets air from the tank on his back.

Seals and sea lions are clever. They can learn tricks. This sea lion learned to balance a ball.

# Whales

Whales are mammals that spend their lives in water. They cannot live on land. Dolphins and porpoises are small whales. A whale's nose is on top of its head. It is called a blowhole. Whales eat fish and shrimps.

dolphin

blue whale

porpoise

sperm whale

narwhal

Greenland whale

killer whale

pilot whale

# MEAT EATERS

Hunting animals that eat meat are called carnivores. They are strong and run fast to catch their prey. They kill their prey with their sharp teeth. Cats, dogs, weasels, and mongooses are carnivores. Large carnivores, such as tigers, sometimes kill people.

The weasel is a small carnivore. But it is very fierce. It can kill animals as big as a rabbit.

The wildcat in the big picture has four long, pointed teeth. These teeth are called canines, or fangs. The wildcat uses its fangs to kill its prey.

The mongoose is famous for killing snakes such as this cobra. The mongoose moves so fast the snake has no time to bite.

The giant panda is a carnivore. But it eats mainly plants. Its favorite food is bamboo. Giant pandas live in China.

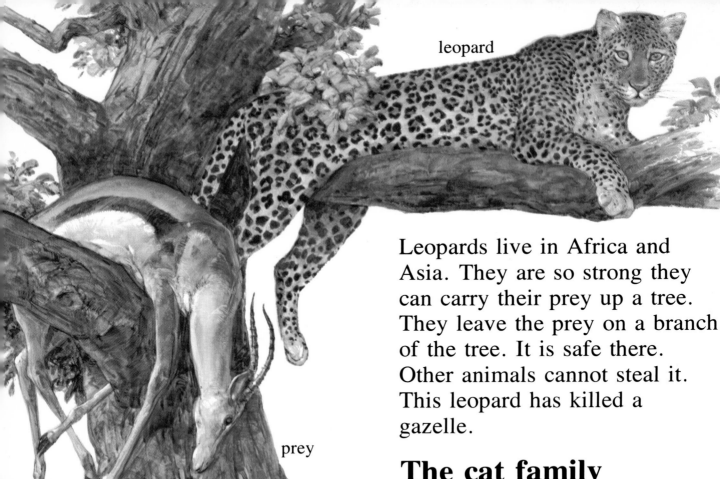

leopard

prey

Leopards live in Africa and Asia. They are so strong they can carry their prey up a tree. They leave the prey on a branch of the tree. It is safe there. Other animals cannot steal it. This leopard has killed a gazelle.

## The cat family

There are about 40 kinds of wildcats. Most of them are small. Five kinds are known as "The Big Cats." They are the lion, tiger, leopard, jaguar, and snow leopard.

Cats usually hunt alone. They wait for their prey, or creep up and jump on it quickly.

Babies of big cats are called cubs. These jaguar cubs are from South America. Baby cats learn to hunt by playing together.

Manx

tabby

Siamese

A lion family is called a pride. Each pride is led by a male lion. He has a large mane of fur. The picture shows a mother lion and her cubs. The females do most of the hunting for the pride.

There are many kinds of pet cats. The tabby looks like the African wildcat that lived long ago. Siamese cats were once kept in temples in Siam, now called Thailand. The Manx cat has long back legs but no tail.

# Dogs and bears

Dogs and bears are carnivores. They are related, but their habits are different. Bears are heavy animals. They walk on the soles of their feet. Dogs walk on their toes. Dogs are good runners. They can go far without getting tired. Dogs are hunters. Wild dogs live in groups called packs.

fox

There are many kinds of dogs. Some dogs are kept as pets. Others must work. This bouvier from Belgium is used to herd cattle.

Bears are carnivores. But most bears eat mainly berries and leaves. They all have long claws. Small bears can climb trees. Bears live alone and sleep all winter. The polar bear lives in the Arctic. It is a good swimmer and hunter. It eats fish and seals.

The fox belongs to the dog family. It hunts alone. It comes out at night to look for mice.

polar bear

This brown bear is feeding her cubs. They were born in her winter den. They came out with her in spring. She will show them how to find food.

# Hoofed mammals

A hoof is a very large toenail. Animals with hoofs stand on tiptoes. Their weight rests on their hoofs.

There are many kinds of hoofed animals. Some, such as the bison and the wildebeest, live in herds. All are plant eaters.

The mouse deer is the smallest kind of hoofed animal. It is only 30 centimeters (about 12 inches) tall. These deer feed at night in their forest home.

Giraffes grow to nearly six meters (almost 20 feet) tall. They live in Africa. They eat the leaves off tall trees.

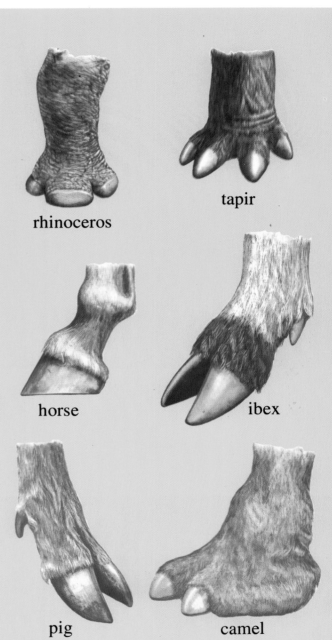

rhinoceros

tapir

horse

ibex

pig

camel

There are two kinds of hoofed animals. One kind has an even number of toes. The other kind has an odd number. Those with two toes are called cloven-hoofed.

## Horses and ponies

Horses have one hoof on each leg. Tame horses often wear special shoes made of iron.

The zebra is a kind of wild horse. It lives in grassy parts of Africa. The zebra is hard to tame.

This animal is a zedonk. One of its parents is a zebra. The other is a donkey.

Wild horses once lived in Europe and Asia. All the horses that we know today came from those wild ones. There are only a few really wild horses left. Some of them roam the range in the western United States. The white horses in the picture on the right run free in the south part of France.

Ponies are small horses. They
often live in wild places. They
are good for riding.

# Deer and antelopes

Deer and antelopes have just two toes on each foot. That is why they are called cloven-hoofed. Male deer have antlers. Most female deer do not. Antlers are made of bone. Each year the antlers drop off. Then the deer grow new ones. The antlers of red deer grow bigger as the animals grow older.

female red deer

antlers

moose

male
red deer

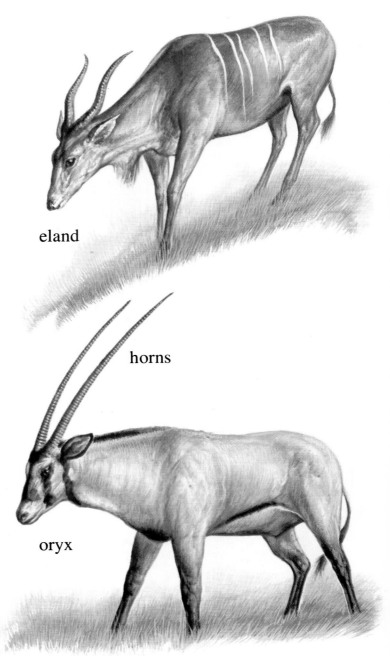

eland

horns

oryx

Thompson's
gazelles

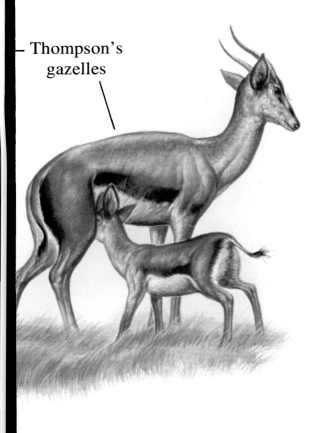

Most antelopes live in Africa.
But there are some in Asia. The
oryx lives in deserts. The
gazelle likes grassy plains. The
largest antelope in the world is
the eland. All antelopes have
horns like those of goats
and cattle.

# Cattle, sheep, and goats

Cattle, sheep, and goats are important because they give us milk, meat, and wool. Long ago people used to hunt wild cattle, sheep, and goats. Now they all are tame.

Goats like the one in the top picture can eat almost anything. They can even climb trees to eat the leaves and bark.

Toggenburg

Kerryhill

Hampshire

British Alpine

British Saarinen

Suffolk

Merino ram

Bison are a kind of wild ox.
They were once hunted in
America for their meat.

Highland

Charolais

Aberdeen Angus

Jersey

Friesian

# Giant mammals

There are giant animals that live on land. They are mammals. The largest one is the African elephant. It is more than three meters (about ten feet) high and weighs more than ten tons. All these giant animals eat plants.

Rhinoceroses can be dangerous. They run very fast. Sometimes they charge at people or cars.

The hippopotamus is found in Africa. It lives in rivers and swamps. It comes to the shore at night to feed. It eats mainly grass.

Indian elephants have smaller ears and tusks than African elephants. They have been tamed for work for many years. They lift tree trunks and other heavy things.

# HOW ANIMALS LIVE

There are many kinds of animals. They have different ways of finding food and looking after their babies. They live in different places and eat different things.

anteaters

There are three kinds of anteaters in South America. The ones in the picture are giant anteaters. They lick up insects with their long sticky tongues. The mother anteater carries its baby on its back. She does this until the baby is quite big.

The gerenuk stands on its back legs to reach high branches.

musk-oxen

52

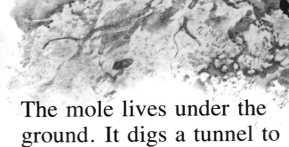

Musk-oxen live in herds in the Arctic. They have thick coats that keep them warm. If a wolf is near, they stand close together so the wolf cannot get their babies. You can see this in the picture below.

The mole lives under the ground. It digs a tunnel to find food.

aye-aye's fingers

The aye-aye's long fingers find insects that live in wood.

# Animals that help us

Our lives would be very different without our tame animals. Such animals have been used for many, many years to help with work. They are used mainly for pulling loads and for riding.

Today, tractors and trucks can do such work. But in some places animals still work.

Sheep dogs are used to herd sheep. The shepherd whistles and tells the dog what to do.

In the Arctic, reindeer pull sleds. They can go far in a day.

Most farmers today use tractors to pull plows. But sometimes horses are still used. The farmer who drives them must be very skillful.

In some places, oxen are used for plowing. They also pull carts. A wooden yoke joins the oxen to the cart.

Camels are used to carry loads and people in the desert. They can go for days without drinking. They do not mind the hot sun. They are also used for plowing.

# Animals of the night

All these animals come out at night. They stay in their homes during the day. We may see them in the evening or when a light shines on them at night. Owls can see well at night. Other animals find their way by hearing.

pipistrell

dormouse

wood mouse

badger

horseshoe bat

tawny owl

fox

hedgehog

# Animal disguise

Many animals hide to protect themselves. They stay very still in the grass. Many have colors that blend with colors in the background. Some can change colors to match different backgrounds. The chameleon can do this. All the animals pictured here are hard to see.

The nightjar nests on the ground. This bird's color makes it hard to see. Can you find it?

Stone curlews hunt for insects at night. During the day they sit on their nests. Their color helps them to hide on the ground.

The cheetah's spots break up the outline of its body. This helps it to hide in the grass.

In the spring, the ptarmigan has brown feathers. The bird is hard to see when it sits on its nest.

In the winter, the ptarmigan has white feathers. You can see two of these birds in the snow.

# Animals in danger

Every year more kinds of animals are in danger of becoming extinct. To become extinct means to die out and never be seen again. Some are killed for their fur. Others are killed because they eat our crops. Some have no home when forests are cut down.

Some animals are protected in special places called reserves. These bison live in such a place.

European bison

Wild asses are hunted for their meat. Only a few now live in the middle of a desert.

The bald eagle is protected. It is the national bird of the United States.

The condor is the largest flying bird. Many condors have been killed by people.

The forests of Borneo and Sumatra are being cut down. That is where orangutans live.

orangutan

# Extinct animals

Many animals will never be seen again. They are now extinct. These animals were hunted until none were left.

Steller's sea cow lived in the Arctic Ocean. It became extinct soon after it was discovered by explorers.

Steller's sea cow

great auk

The last great auk was seen in Iceland 100 years ago. Great auks could not fly. So they were easily killed for food.

The Tasmanian wolf lived in Australia. Ranchers hunted it because it killed sheep.

Tasmanian wolf

giant aurochs

The giant aurochs once lived in Europe. Our cattle came from this animal family.

quagga

Herds of quaggas lived in South Africa. They were hunted for meat. They are now extinct.

# GLOSSARY

These words are defined the way they are used in the book.

**agouti** (uh GOO tee) a mammal that looks and acts like a rabbit

**ancestor** (AN ses tuhr) a person from whom one is descended

**anteater** (ANT ee tur) a mammal with a long, thin nose that eats ants

**antelope** (AN tuh lohp) a cloven-hoofed mammal with horns

**antlers** (ANT lurs) branched horns found on deer, elk or moose

**ape** (ayp) an animal like a large monkey with little or no tail

**armadillo** (AHR muh *DIL* oh) a mammal with bony plates in its upper skin

**armor** (ARM ur) a hard covering used for protection

**auk** (awk) a sea bird that swims very well but is a poor flyer

**auroch** (AWR ahk) a wild ox once found in Europe; it is now extinct

**aye-aye** (EYE eye) a small squirrel-like animal

**baboon** (ba BOON) a large monkey that lives mostly on the ground

**bald eagle** (bawld EE g'l) a large North American eagle with white head feathers

**beak** (beek) the hard mouth part of a bird

**beaver** (BEEV uhr) a furry, gnawing mammal with a wide flat tail

**bilby** (BIHL bee) a pouched mammal that lives in a burrow and has long ears like a rabbit

**bird of paradise** (burd uhv PAIR uh dys) a colorful bird of hot forests

**bird of prey** (burd uhv pray) a bird that hunts and eats other animals

**bison** (BY s'n) a cloven-hoofed wild ox

**blowholes** (BLOH hohls) a whale's nostrils or breathing holes

**burrow** (BUR oh) an underground home

**camel** (KA mehl) a large, strong mammal found in the desert

**canine** (KAY nyn) the four, long, pointed teeth found in carnivores

**carnivore** (KAHR nih vohr) an animal that eats meat

**cattle** (KAT uhl) a cloven-hoofed mammal important for its milk or meat

**chameleon** (kuh MEE lee uhn) a lizard that changes its skin color to help hide

**chick** (chihk) a baby bird

**chimpanzee** (CHIM pan *ZEE*) an ape that lives mostly on the ground

**cloven-hoofed** (KLOHV uhn hufd) a hoofed animal with two toes

**condor** (KAHN dohr) the largest flying bird

**crane** (krayn) the largest long-legged water bird

**crested pigeon** (KREHST uhd PIJ uhn) a bird with a tuft of feathers on its head

**deer** (deer) a cloven-hoofed mammal with antlers

**diatryma** (DY uh *TRY* muh) a large meat-eating bird that lived about 60 million years ago

**disguise** (dihs GYZ) to change or hide the way one looks

**dolphin** (DAHL fuhn) a small toothed sea mammal that belongs to the whale family

**domestic** (DUH *MEHS* tihk) tamed and able to be used by people

**echidna** (ee KID nuh) a mammal that lays eggs

**eland** (EE lund) the largest antelope in Africa

**elephant** (EHL uh fuhnt) A huge land mammal with large ears and a long nose called a trunk

**extinct** (ehks TIHNGKT) to die out and never be seen again

**feather** (FEHTH uhr) one of the light growths that cover a bird's skin

**flamingo** (fluh MIHNG goh) a long-legged water bird with a curved bill and long neck

**flock** (flahk) many birds grouped together

**foal** (fohl) a young horse

**fulmar** (FOOL mur) a sea bird that stays near shore to nest and hunt for food

**gaggle** (GAG gehl) a flock of geese on the ground

**gannet** (GAN neht) a large, white sea bird with black-tipped wings

**gazelle** (guh ZEHL) a cloven-hoofed antelope that lives on grassy plains

**gerbil** (JUR buhl) a small, furry rodent that lives in the desert but is often kept as a pet

**gerenuk** (JUR eh nuk) an antelope that stands on its back legs to eat leaves on high branches

**giant panda** (JY uhnt PAN duh) a large black and white bear-like animal from Asia

**gibbon** (GIB uhn) the smallest ape; it swings through trees by its arms

**giraffe** (juh RAF) a tall four-legged mammal with a long neck and spots on its skin

**gnawing mammal** (NAW ihng MAM uhl) a mammal with sharp, strong teeth which it uses to gnaw or bite its food

**gorilla** (gawr IH la) a large ape that lives mainly on the ground

**goshawk** (GAHS hawk) a bird of prey that lives in forests

**gull** (guhl) a long-winged sea bird

**hamster** (HAM stuhr) a small, furry rodent that is sometimes kept as a pet

**hare** (hehr) a small, furry gnawing animal with long ears and strong hind legs

**hawfinch** (HAW fihnch) a bird with a strong, pointed beak

**hawk** (hawk) a bird of prey with a sharp, hooked beak, strong claws and short rounded wings

**heron** (HEHR uhn) a long-legged water bird with a sharply pointed bill

**hippopotamus** (HIHP uh *PAHT* uh muhs) a large land mammal that lies in the water during the day and comes on land at night to feed

**hoof** (huf) a very large toenail

**jaguar** (JAG wahr) one of the largest, most powerful wild cats

**jerboa** (jur BOH uh) a small rodent that looks like a kangaroo

**kangaroo** (KANG uh *ROO*) a pouched mammal that hops with both legs together

**kittiwake** (KIHT ih wayk) a sea bird that makes its nest on cliffs

**kiwi** (KEE wee) a New Zealand bird that cannot fly

**koala** ( koh AH luh) a pouched mammal that looks like a bear and is found in Australia

**lemming** (LEHM ihng) a small furry rodent hunted by owls for food

**leopard** (LEHP uhrd) a large, spotted member of the cat family

**lioness** (LY uhn ehs) a female lion

**lodge** (lahj) a beaver's home

which is built of wood and leaves near water

**mallard** (MAL uhrd) a duck with a flat, round beak

**mammal** (MAM uhl) a warm-blooded animal that feeds milk to its young

**mandarin** (MAN duh rihn) a duck that builds its nest on the ground near water

**mane** (mayn) the long, thick hair found on certain animals

**Manx** (manx) a type of pet cat that has long back legs but no tail

**merganser** (muhr GAN suhr) a duck with a special hooked beak used to hold slippery fish

**migrate** (MY grayt) the movement of people or animals from one place to another

**moa** (MOH uh) a bird with a long neck and legs that is now extinct

**mole** (mohl) a small, plump mammal that lives underground

**mongoose** (MAHN goos) a small carnivore famous for killing snakes

**monkey** (MUNG kee) a mammal that climbs trees with its legs and arms

**mouse deer** (mows deer) the smallest hoofed mammal

**musk oxen** (musk OKS uhn) a shaggy, slow, clumsy-looking mammal

**nightjar** (NYT jahr) a bird that nests on the ground

**opossum** (uh PAHS uhm) a small, pouched mammal found in North America

**orangutan** (oh RANG oo tan) a large ape with long arms for climbing

**oryx** (OHR iks) a cloven-hoofed antelope that lives in the desert

**osprey** (AHS pree) a large bird of prey that eats only fish

**otter** (AHT uhr) a furry mammal that swims very fast in water

**owl** (owl) a bird of prey that hunts at night

**owlet** (OWL eht) a baby owl

**ox** (oks) a large shaggy mammal with horns

**oxen** (OKS uhn) the plural of ox

**parrot** (PAIR uht) a bright, colorful bird found mainly in warm areas of the world

**peacock** (PEE kahk) a large, beautiful bird with a colorful tail

**peahen** (PEE hehn) a female peacock

**pest** (pehst) animals that live in large numbers and cause damage

**piglet** (PIHG leht) a baby pig

**platypus** (PLAT uh puhs) a mammal that lays eggs

**pony** (POH nee) a small horse

**porpoise** (PAWR pus) another name for a dolphin

**pouched mammal** (pawchd MAM uhl) a mammal with a large pocket to carry its baby in

**prey** (pray) an animal that is hunted and eaten by another animal

**pride** (pryd) a group or family of lions

**ptarmigan** (TAR muh gan) a bird with short feathers on its feet

**puffin** (PUHF ihn) a sea bird that nests in burrows in cliffs

**quagga** (KWAG uh) a horse-like animal, now extinct, that lived in South Africa

**rabbit** (RAB iht) a furry, gnawing mammal, with long ears and a short, fluffy tail

**ram** (ram) a male sheep

**reindeer** (RAYN deer) a deer that lives in northern Europe and Asia

**reserve** (reh SURV) a special place where animals are protected

**rhinoceros** (ry NAHS ur uhs) a huge, horned mammal with thick, loose skin covering a solid body and short legs

**robin** (RAHB ihn) a song bird. The male has bright orange-red feathers on its breast

**rodent** (ROH dehnt) a gnawing mammal

**sea lion** (SEE ly uhn) a sea mammal with flippers on its side and tail

**sheepdog** (SHEEP dawg) a dog trained to herd sheep

**shoveler** (SHUHV ehl ur) a duck with a spoon-shaped bill

**shrew** (shroo) a tiny mammal with a sharp nose

**Siamese** (SY uh mees) a type of pet cat with blue eyes and dark fur on its head, paws and tail

**skein** (skayn) a flock of geese in the air

**skunk** (skuhnk) a small furry mammal with black and white markings. When frightened, it sprays a bad-smelling liquid

**sloth** (slohth) a slow-moving tree mammal

**Steller's seacow** (STEHL urs SEE kow) a large mammal that once lived in the Arctic Ocean; it is now extinct

**stone curlew** (stohn KUR loo) a bird that hunts for insects at night

**stork** (stawrk) a long-legged bird that often nests on roofs and chimneys

**swan** (swahn) the largest of waterfowl; it has white feathers and a long neck

**tabby** (TAB ee) a type of pet cat with dark stripes and white fur

**Tasmanian wolf** (taz MAY nee uhn wuhlf) A mammal that looks like a long-tailed, striped dog. It is rarely seen today

**tern** (turn) a sea bird that stays near shore to hunt and nest

**turkey** (TUR kee) a large North American bird that is hunted in the autumn

**tusk** (tuhsk) a long, pointed tooth that sticks out of the head of certain animals

**vole** (vohl) a mouse-like rodent

**vulture** (vuhl chuhr) a bird of prey that usually eats dead animals

**wallaby** (WAWL uh bee) a small kangaroo that can hop very fast

**walrus** (WAWL ruhs) a sea mammal with tusks

**warm-blooded** (WAWRM bluhd ihd) having blood that stays at almost the same temperature, even when the temperature of the air or surroundings changes

**wandering albatross** (WAHND ur ihng *AL* buh TRAWS) a sea bird that flies far out to sea to hunt

**waterfowl** (WAW tuhr fowl) a bird that lives near lakes, rivers or ponds

**weasel** (WEE zehl) a small carnivore with a long slender body and short legs

**webbed feet** (wehbd feet) feet in which the toes are joined together

**whale** (hwayl) a huge sea mammal with blow holes on its head to breathe through

**wildebeest** (WIHL deh beest) a hoofed mammal of Africa

**woodpecker** (WUD pehk uhr) a bird that uses its strong beak to make holes in trees in search of insects

**zebra** (ZEE bruh) a striped, horse-like mammal found in Africa

**zedonk** (ZEE dahnk) an animal that has a zebra for one parent and a donkey for another

# FURTHER READING

Anderson, John Merrick. *The Changing World of Birds*. New York: Holt, Rinehart and Winston, 1973. 122pp.

Ardley, Neil. *Birds*. New York: Warwick Press, 1976. 48pp.

Austin, Elizabeth S. *The Random House Book of Birds*. New York: Random House, 1970. 131pp.

Board, Tessa. *Birds.* New York: F. Watts, 1983.

Board, Tessa. *Mammals.* New York: F. Watts, 1983.

Cochrane, Jennifer. *Secrets of Nature.* Windermere, Florida: Rourke, 1981.

Cox, Rosamund Kidman. *Birds.* Tulsa, Oklahoma: Usborne Publishing, 1980.

Davidson, Margaret. *Wild Animal Families.* New York: Hastings House, 1980.

Friskey, Margaret. *Birds We Know.* Chicago: Childrens Press, 1981.

Hicks, J. L. *A Closer Look at Birds.* New York: F. Watts, 1976. 30pp.

Jacobs, Francine. *Bermudapetrel: The Bird That Would Not Die.* New York: Morrow, 1981.

Johnson, Burdetta F. *African Lions and Cats.* New York: D. McKay Company, 1969. 182pp.

Johnson, Sylvia A. *Animals of Deserts.* Minneapolis: Lerner Publications Company, 1976. 28pp.

Johnson, Sylvia A. *Animals of the Grasslands.* Minneapolis: Lerner Publications Company, 1976. 28pp.

Johnson, Sylvia A. *Animals of the Mountains*.
Minneapolis: Lerner Publications Company,
1976. 28pp.

Johnson, Sylvia A. *Animals of the Polar
Regions*. Minneapolis: Lerner Publications
Company, 1976. 28pp.

Johnson, Sylvia A. *Animals of the Temperate
Forests*. Minneapolis: Lerner Publications
Company, 1976. 28pp.

Johnson, Sylvia A. *Animals of the Tropical
Forests*. Minneapolis: Lerner Publications
Company, 1976. 28pp.

Laycock, George. *Wingspread: A World of
Birds*. New York: Four Winds Press, 1972.
125pp.

Lowery, Barbara. *Mammals*. New York:
F. Watts, 1976. 47pp.

Peterson, Roger. *The Birds*. Young Readers
Ed. New York: Time, Inc., 1967. 128pp.

Reidel, Marlene. *From Egg to Bird.*
Minneapolis: Carolrhoda Books, 1981.

Silverstein, Alvin. *Mammals of the Sea*.
San Carlos, California: Golden Gate Junior
Books, 1971. 89pp.

Storms, Laura. *The Bird Book.* Minneapolis:
Lerner Publications, 1982.

Stoutenburg, Adrien. *Animals at Bay: Rare
and Rescued American Wildlife*. Garden
City, New York: Doubleday, 1968. 159pp.

Taylor, Anne. *Farm Animals.* Windermere,
Florida: Rourke, 1981.

Vevers, Henry G. *Birds and Their Nests*.
New York: McGraw-Hill, 1973. 32pp.

# QUESTIONS TO THINK ABOUT

## Warm-Blooded Animals

**Do you remember?**

There are two kinds of warm-blooded animals. What are they called?

What kind of animal has a fur coat?

What is a bird's coat made of?

How do the coats of birds and mammals help these animals?

When do some warm-blooded animals grow a thicker coat? How does this help the animals?

**Find out about . . .**

The ways birds and mammals are different. Name three of these ways.

Mammals that live underground. Do they stay underground all the time? What do they eat?

Warm-blooded animals that make good pets. Can you name two kinds of birds that people keep as pets? Name three mammal pets.

## Birds

**Do you remember?**

What do tree birds eat?

Not all birds live in trees. Where else do they live?

Some birds hunt and eat other animals. What are these birds called?

What seabird makes its nest of seaweed high on the cliffs?

How are long-legged birds helped by their long legs? How are they helped by their long necks?

**Find out about . . .**

The hummingbird. How big is it? Where does it live? What does it eat?

The swan. What kind of bird is it? How does it live? How is its long neck useful?

Birds that cannot fly. Why are the kiwi and ostrich not able to fly? In what ways are these birds different from the birds that you know?

# Mammals

**Do you remember?**

How many kinds of mammals are there?

How do mammals feed their babies?

Two kinds of mammals lay eggs. Name them.

What is a pouched mammal? Name one.

There are four kinds of apes. Name two.

How do the long arms of gibbons and orangutans help these animals?

**Find out about . . .**

The flying mammal. What is its name? Where does it live? When and how does it eat?

The way mammals care for their babies. Are all baby mammals helpless at birth? Do the babies of pouched mammals need the most care?

The sloth. How does it travel through its forest home?

Apes and monkeys. How are the bodies of apes different from the bodies of monkeys? Do monkeys and apes eat the same kinds of food?

# Gnawing Mammals

**Do you remember?**

Some gnawing mammals are called rodents. Name two well-known rodent pests.

Why can rodents eat hard nuts and roots?

How are the teeth of rabbits and hares different from the teeth of rodents?

Some kinds of rodents are often kept as pets. Name two of them.

Beavers are gnawing mammals that cut down trees. Why do they do this? How do they use the trees?

The damage done by rats and mice. Why are these rodents harmful? What must people do to control rats and mice?

The Arctic hare. Why can this animal hide from its enemies?

The value of beavers to people. How do the dams that beavers build prevent flooding? When trappers kill many beavers, what happens to the land?

# Sea Mammals

**Do you remember?**

What are the names of four kinds of sea mammals?

Often certain sea mammals come to shore. Why do they do this?

How do sea lions and walruses move fast on land?

How does a whale's tail help it?

What do whales eat?

**Find out about . . .**

How seals and sea lions are trained. What kinds of tricks can they do? How are they rewarded for doing them?

Porpoises and dolphins. Why are scientists

studying them? How smart are these sea mammals?

The whale's blowhole. How does it help the whale?

How sea mammals keep warm. What keeps these animals from freezing to death in the cold sea?

# Meat Eaters

**Do you remember?**

What are carnivores? Name three of them.

What special body parts help carnivores get their food?

How are a wildcat's teeth different from your teeth? Would your kind of teeth help a wildcat?

Name three members of the cat family.

How are dogs and bears related? How are they different?

**Find out about . . .**

How wild carnivores live. How do lions in Africa get their food? Why do people in India hunt and kill tigers? How do wolves in Alaska live in winter?

Coyotes in America. Why are they a problem? How do they hunt? How do people feel about them?

Weasels and mongooses. What do these small carnivores look like? What do they eat? Are they more helpful to people than harmful?

# Hoofed Mammals

**Do you remember?**

What is a hoof? How do hoofs help animals?

What do hoofed animals eat?

What is the name of the smallest hoofed animal? How tall is it?

How are horses and ponies alike? How are they different?

What are antlers? What are they made of?

Cows, sheep, and goats are cloven-hoofed. What does that mean?

Name three large hoofed animals.

**Find out about . . .**

The African wildebeest. How does it live? Who are its enemies? How does it escape from its enemies?

Giraffes. How do they drink water? Does the giraffe's long neck help it in any way?

The kinds of horses. Read about many different kinds of horses. What are they used for? Where can we find wild horses? How can they be tamed?

# How Animals Live

**Do you remember?**

What is unusual about the way an anteater cares for its baby?

How do muskoxen protect their babies from attacks by wolves?

Name three animals that help people. How do they help?

Where do night animals stay during the day?

The ptarmigan can always hide from its enemies. Why is this true?

How are people trying to keep the bison from becoming extinct?

**Find out about . . .**

The mole and how it lives. What does it eat?

Camels. How do people use them?

Kangaroos. Where do they live? How fast can they run?

The bald eagle. Why is it in danger?

# PROJECTS

**Project — Cold Climate Animals**

Look up in encyclopedias and other books how animals live in cold places. Make a list of those that live in Alaska and other parts of the Arctic. Put a circle around those you think are warm-blooded.

Make a chart for these warm-blooded animals. Put the name of each animal in the first column of your chart. In a second column, to the right of the name, write what you think keeps this animal warm in winter. In a third column, write words that tell what body parts help this animal get food. Also, write words that tell how it protects itself against enemies.

**Project — Animals Around You**

Look around you and find out what warm-blooded animals live in your neighborhood. How many can you actually see? Can you see where they live? Do you think that other animals that you cannot see also live near you? Are they warm-blooded? Use the library to help you decide.

Make a list of all these warm-blooded animals. Divide the list into birds and mammals. Put a star by each one you have seen. Then write what each starred one looks like.

# INDEX

**Photo Credits:** B.&C. Alexander; Heather Angel M. Sc., F.R.P.S.; J. Allan Cash; Bruce Coleman; Brian Hawkes; Geoffrey Kinns; Pat Morris; Natural History Photography Agency; G.R. Roberts; Royal Society for the Protection of Birds; S.A. Thompson; ZEFA.

**Front cover:** K. Jell, B. Sandved.

**Illustrators:** Fred Anderson; John Barber; Gill Embleton: Elizabeth Graham-Yool; Richard Hook; Eric Jewell; Steve King; Pat Lenander; Vanessa Luff; George Thompson; Mike Whelply.